W9-CKI-507

Have Fun with

Arts

and

Crafts

Knights

and Castles

Rita Storey

A⁺
Smart Apple Media

Published by Smart Apple Media,
an imprint of Black Rabbit Books
P.O. Box 3263, Mankato, Minnesota 56002
www.blackrabbitbooks.com

Published by arrangement with the Watts
Publishing Group LTD, London.

Library of Congress Cataloging-in-Publication Data

Storey, Rita. Knights and castles / Rita Storey.
pages cm. — (Have fun with arts and crafts)
Includes index.
Summary: "Learn about dragons, jousting, and jesters as you create
your own coat of arms, armor, catapult, and more! Easy to follow directions and
supply lists included for each craft" –Provided by publisher.
ISBN 978-1-59920-899-2 (library binding)
1. Handicraft—Juvenile literature. 2. Knights and knighthood—Juvenile literature.
3. Civilization, Medieval—Juvenile literature. I. Title.
TT157.S8257 2014
745.5—dc23
2012030575

Packaged for Franklin Watts by Storeybooks
rita@storeybooks.co.uk
Designer: Rita Storey
Editor: Nicola Barber
Crafts: Rita Storey
Photography: Tudor Photography, Banbury
www.tudorphotography.co.uk

Cover images: Shutterstock (top left), Tudor Photography, Banbury

Before You Start

Some of the projects in this book require scissors, paint, glue, and a sewing
needle. When using these things, we recommend that children are supervised by
a responsible adult. When a project requires the use of a craft knife (pages 4–5,
8–9, and 12–13), it must be used by a responsible adult.

Printed in the United States
at Corporate Graphics,
North Mankato, Minnesota
PO1588
2-2013

9 8 7 6 5 4 3 2 1

Contents

Medieval Castle

In the Middle Ages, knights lived in castles with thick, stone walls and tall towers. You can make your own fantastic castle complete with battlements, towers, and a gatehouse to keep out the fiercest army.

For a castle stronghold, you will need

- a craft knife (ask an adult to use the knife)
- large cardboard box
- 4 large cardboard potato chip tubes
- ruler
- paint
- paintbrush
- small cardboard box
- 2 cardboard tubes from inside a paper towel roll
- thin silver card stock
- double-sided tape
- tape
- glue
- scissors
- colored paper and toothpicks to make the flags

1 Using the scissors or the craft knife, cut the top off the large cardboard box so that the sides are 1½ in. (4 cm) shorter than the cardboard chip tubes. Cut down each corner of the box to make four flaps as shown.

Cardboard can be hard to cut, so ask a grownup to help you with this.

2 Cut a strip ¾ in. (2 cm) wide off both sides of each flap. Paint both sides of the flaps of the opened-out cardboard box. Allow it to dry.

3 Paint the four potato chip tubes, the small box, and the two smaller tubes. Allow it to dry.

4 To make the tops of the towers, or battlements, cut four strips of silver cardstock long enough to wrap around a potato chip tube. The strips should be 1 in (3 cm) wide. Cut rectangles out of the top of each strip, equally spaced to look like the ones in this picture. Use double-sided tape to attach a strip to the top of each tube.

4

5 Cut four strips of silver cardstock the same length as the four sides of the large cardboard box. Each strip should be 1 in. (2.5 cm) wide. Then follow the instructions in step 4 to cut out the battlements. Glue a strip to the top of each side of the large box.

6 Cut two strips of cardstock long enough to wrap around a small tube. Each strip should be ½ in. (1½ cm) wide. Cut small rectangles out of the top edge of each strip (see step 4). Using double-sided tape, attach a strip to the top of each of the small tubes.

7 Using tape, attach the four potato chip tubes to the four corners of the box. Make sure the tape is on the inside of the box so it does not show.

8 Glue the small cardboard box to the middle of the front of the castle. This will be your gatehouse. Glue a small cardboard tube on either side of the small box.

Get ready to protect your castle against the enemy!

9 Paint narrow windows on the towers. Cut strips of silver cardstock and glue them together to make a portcullis. Shape the top to look like the one in the picture. Glue it onto the gatehouse.

10 Use the template on page 31 to cut out flags from folded colored paper. Place the short, straight edge of the template on the fold on your paper. Open the flags, spread glue on them and fold each one over a toothpick. Attach them to the inside of the towers with tape.

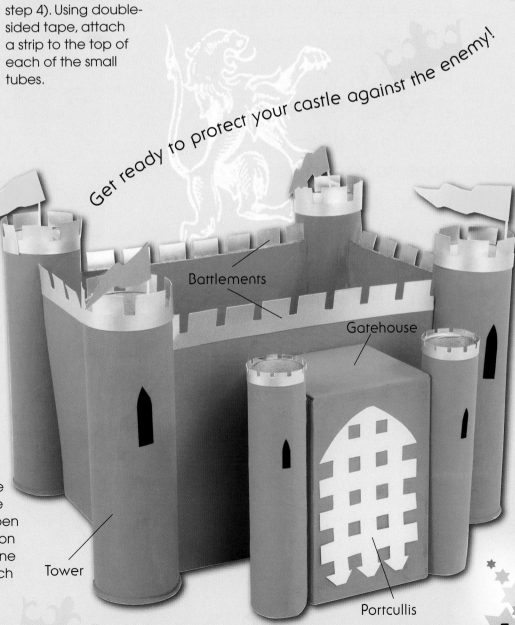

Battlements

Gatehouse

Tower

Portcullis

Coat of Arms

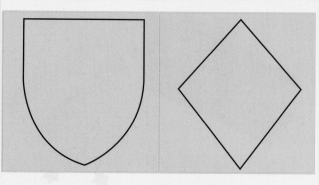

A coat of arms is a design made up of shapes and symbols. A knight had his own coat of arms on his shield and tunic. His followers wore his coat of arms too. In battle, a coat of arms was useful for showing who was fighting on which side—it was hard to recognize people wearing helmets and armor! Create your own coat of arms to hang on your bedroom door.

For a coat of arms design, you will need

- large sheets of paper
- scissors
- ruler
- glue
- felt pens, pencils, or crayons
- paints and paintbrushes
- gold or silver paint
- colored paper

1 Choose a shape for your coat of arms and draw it on the large sheet of paper. Cut it out.

2 Paint or color the whole shape or divide it into sections like the ones shown above. Then paint or color the sections in two contrasting colors.

3 Paint a cross, a thick stripe, or a chevron with either gold or silver paint on a large piece of paper. Allow it to dry. Using your coat of arms shape as a guide, cut out the stripe or chevron so it will fit your shape. Glue it to your coat of arms shape.

4 Think of some pictures that tell other people about your hobbies and interests. Draw a symbol for each one on the colored paper and cut out the shapes.

5 Glue the symbols on to the gold or silver part of your design.

6 Copy the helmet design from the template on page 32. Add it to your coat of arms to show that you are a knight.

Coat of Arms Design

The design of every coat of arms is unique to its owner. By looking at a coat of arms, an expert can learn a lot about who owns it. Today, schools, universities, and other organizations often have coats of arms. Your school may have one.

Defend Yourself

When a knight went into battle, he carried a strong shield for protection from swords and arrows. Make this awesome shield and get ready to defend yourself.

To make this sturdy shield, you will need

- large sheet of paper
- pencil
- scissors
- big piece of poster board
- craft knife (ask an adult to use it)
- ruler
- glue
- 4 sheets of colored paper, 2 of each color
- silver duct tape
- strong cardstock

1 Fold the paper in half. Starting at the fold, draw the shape of half a shield on the paper. Cut along the line you have drawn and open out the shape.

2 Draw around the shape on to the board. Ask an adult to cut out the shape using a sharp craft knife.

3 Using a ruler, divide the shield into four quarters.

4 Cover the front of the shield with glue and place a piece of paper on to each quarter of the shield. Use the lines you have drawn to line up your paper.

5 Turn the shape over and carefully trim off the excess paper.

6 Use silver duct tape to make a cross in the center of the shield. The cross should stretch from top to bottom and from the left to right. Copy two shapes from page 30 twice on to the leftover pieces of colored paper. Cut them out. Glue one on each quarter of the shield. If you prefer, you can use your own coat of arms design (see pages 6–7).

7 Cut a piece of cardstock 1½ in. (4 cm) shorter than the width of the top of the shield and 4 in. (10 cm) wide. Cut two strips of cardstock, each one long enough to go around your arm with a little room to spare. Tape them into circles. Attach the circles to the piece of cardstock with duct tape.

8 Tape this cardboard panel as close as possible to each edge on the back of the shield. Because the panel is shorter than the width of the shield it will make the shield curve a bit. Slide your arm through one circle and hold on to the other.

Have your shield ready to stop any swords that may come your way.

From Page to Squire

Boys chosen to train as knights usually left home at the age of seven. They became pages (assistants) to grand knights and lived in their castles. Pages had a lot to learn. They were taught good manners and how to read and write. At the age of 14, pages became squires. This was when they began to learn the skills of fighting and jousting.

A Knight's Helmet

This fearsome helmet will frighten your enemies and protect your head at the same time. Knights wore helmets to fend off cuts from swords and knives.

To make a knight's helmet, you will need

- compass
- felt-tip pen
- silver cardstock
- scissors
- ruler
- tape
- gold paper
- glue

1 Open the compass to 4 in. (10 cm) and draw a circle on the back of the silver cardstock. Draw a triangle out of the top of the circle to make a teardrop shape.

2 Draw a line ½ in. (1 cm) outside the edge of the teardrop shape and cut out along this line.

3 Cut triangular slits from the outside to the inner line to make tabs all around the shape.

4 Using a ruler, draw two lines from the middle of the circle (where the compass point was) to the outside of the circle, about 2 in. (5 cm) apart and directly opposite the point on the shape. Cut out the triangle between these two lines.

5 Bend the tabs down along the original outline.

6 Bring the straight edges together and fasten at the back with tape to make a cone shape.

7 To make the main part of the helmet, cut a rectangle of silver cardstock about 9 in. (20 cm) by 27½ in. (70 cm). Fold it in half and shape the top edge as shown above. Decide where you want your eye slits to be. Cut out the two slits.

8 Open out the cardstock. Fit the fold to the triangle on the cone of the headpiece. Tape the tabs onto the inside of the main part of the helmet. Tape the back of the helmet together.

9 Copy the shape on page 30 on to gold paper. Make three of these shapes and tape them on to the points of the helmet. Cut out two thick cross shapes from gold paper. Round off the corners and glue the shapes on to the sides of the helmet.

Your scary helmet will frighten off enemies.

To become a full-fledged knight, make the sword on pages 12–13 to go with your shield and helmet.

From Squire to Knight

When a squire became a knight he was given the title "Sir" in front of his name. Today, some countries still reward bravery or loyal service by making people knights. In the United Kingdom, a special "knighting" ceremony is held at New Year's and on the queen's official birthday. The person to be knighted kneels before the queen, who touches both their shoulders with a ceremonial sword.

A Fine Sword

O n the battlefield, knights often carried big swords called broadswords. This type of sword was so heavy that a knight had to hold it with both hands to swing it around and fight with it. A broadsword had sharp edges and a pointed tip. This sword looks the same—but it is a lot less dangerous!

To make this fine fighting sword, you will need

- side of a cardboard box 6 in. x 20 in. (15 cm x 50 cm)
- felt-tip pen
- scissors or craft knife (ask an adult to use it)
- thick cardstock
- glue
- roll of wide duct tape
- ribbon
- stick-on jewels

1 Draw the blade of a sword on the cardboard. Cut it out. Use this cutout as a template to draw around and make a second, identical shape.

2 Draw the handle of a sword on a piece of cardstock. It should be abo a quarter of the length of y sword blade. Cut it out. Use cutout as a template to dra around and make a secon identical shape.

3 Spread glue on one of the blade shapes and stick the other one on top of it.

4 Glue one of the handle pieces to the top of the blade. Then spread glue all over the rest of the handle and glue the second piece on top, sandwiching the blade in the middle.

5 Tape the edges of the handle together to make sure they are secured. Tightly wrap the whole sword in silver duct tape.

6 Spread glue on both sides of the guard. Wrap ribbon around the guard. Allow it to dry.

7 Decorate the guard with stick-on jewels.

Grip

Guard

Use this sword wisely like a brave knight.

Blade

The Tales of King Arthur

No one knows who King Arthur really was, but the tales written about him and his brave band of knights are very famous.

One story is about the magic sword, Excalibur. The sword lies buried deep in a stone. The person who can pull it out is the rightful king of Britain. Arthur comes across the stone just at the moment when he needs a sword. Everyone is amazed when he pulls it out easily. Arthur becomes a great king and rules very wisely.

You could make a smaller version of this sword to use as a dagger.

Ready for Battle

Knights often wore chainmail to go into battle. Over the top, a knight wore a tunic with his coat of arms on it. You can wear this fantastic chainmail shirt and tunic with your helmet, shield, and sword to complete your knight's outfit.

To make chainmail and a tunic, you will need

For the chainmail
- 2 gray, long-sleeved T-shirts
- piece of cardstock
- black fabric paint
- tray
- bottle cap
- Velcro
- glue
- scissors

For the tunic
- fleece fabric
  15¾ in. x 47 in. (40 cm x 120 cm)
- felt
- glue
- bathrobe belt

1 Lay one of the T-shirts on a flat surface.

2 Pour some black paint into the tray. Spread it out using the piece of cardstock. Dip the bottle cap in the paint and stamp circles on to the sleeves of the T-shirt. Overlap the prints to make them look like chainmail. Keep doing this until you have covered the front of the T-shirt and the front of the sleeves. Allow it to dry.

3 Turn the T-shirt over and repeat step 2 on the back of the T-shirt.

4 For the chainmail collar, cut a circle out of the second T-shirt. Cut a small hole in the center. Follow step 2 to stamp on the chainmail pattern. Allow it to dry.

5 Cut the circle open. Stick a piece of Velcro to the two sides as shown.

6 To make the tunic, fold the length of fleece fabric in half. Cut a scoop from the folded edge so that it will fit over your head.

7 Cut out a shield shape from the felt. Copy the template on page 32 for a lion. Glue it on to the front of the tunic.

8 Put on the chainmail T-shirt. Wear the tunic over the top and use the bathrobe belt to secure it. Put the collar around your neck and fasten it together. With your sword (pages 12–13), shield (pages 8–9), and helmet (pages 10–11), you are now ready to go into battle!

Chivalry

Knights followed a set of rules called the "code of chivalry." Before a squire could become a knight, he had to promise to be honest, brave, and loyal, to protect people weaker than himself, and to fight for the good of everyone—not just for himself.

15

Knight's Castle Card

A knight's castle often had a water-filled moat around it to keep out attackers. A drawbridge was raised and lowered across the moat to let people in and out. This card has a drawbridge surprise.

For a knight's castle card, you will need

- thin cardstock
  12 in. x 6 in. (30 cm x 15 cm)
- colored paper
- wrapping paper
- felt-tip pen
- scissors
- glue
- a small photograph of you or your family
- hole punch
- sharp pencil
- thin ribbon
- glitter

1 Fold the cardstock in half. Use the templates on page 31 to cut three towers from the colored paper, and five window shapes and a gatehouse from the wrapping paper. Glue the shapes on to the front of the card.

2 Glue the photograph in the middle of the gatehouse ½ in. (1 cm) from the bottom. Draw window panes onto the window shapes.

3 To make the drawbridge, cut a rectangle of cardstock the same size as your photograph plus ½ in. (1 cm) all the way around. Shape it so that the top is slightly narrower than the bottom. Bend back ½ in. (1 cm) of the cardstock at the bottom to make a flap.

4 Punch a hole in each of the top two corners of the drawbridge. Put some glue on the colored side of the flap and stick it down just under the photograph. When the drawbridge is folded up, it should cover the photograph.

5 Close your drawbridge and use the holes you have made in the drawbridge as a guide to make holes in the gatehouse with a sharp pencil.

6 Cut two lengths of ribbon and tie a knot in the end of each one. Start at the front of the card with the drawbridge up. Thread one piece of ribbon through one of the drawbridge holes and then through the hole in the gatehouse. Do the same on the other side of the drawbridge.

7 Allow enough ribbon for the drawbridge to open fully. Then tie a knot inside the card and cut off any extra ribbon.

Lower the drawbridge to see who is living in the castle.

8 You can decorate your castle with glitter. Write a message inside your card and pull up the drawbridge.

Crazy Catapult

Castle walls were so thick and strong that it was almost impossible to break them down. Instead, armies did a lot of damage by catapulting missiles over the walls. This fun catapult fires silver foil boulders.

To make a crazy catapult, you will need

- cardboard tube from a paper towel roll
- wrapping paper
- 12 in. (30 cm) ruler
- silver duct tape
- 3 in. (7.5 cm) rubber band
- matchbox tray
- paint and paintbrush
- double-sided tape
- aluminum foil
- cotton balls
- tape

1 Glue wrapping paper on to the tube. Cover the ruler with duct tape.

2 Loop the two ends of the rubber band around the tube.

3 Pass one end of the rubber band through the other. Hold the loop with your finger.

4 Push the ruler through the loop that you are holding. The rubber band should be a quarter of the way along the ruler.

5 Paint the matchbox tray. Allow it to dry.

6 Use double-sided tape to stick the painted box to the end of the ruler farthest away from the tube.

7 Make some ammunition to launch from your catapult by scrunching aluminum foil around cotton balls to make boulders.

8 Tape the ends of the tube to a work surface. Load a boulder into the box.

9 Take aim and FIRE! Press down quickly on the end of the ruler that is opposite to the box.

Trebuchet

In the Middle Ages, one way of attacking a castle was to use a machine called a trebuchet. This was a clever type of catapult that used weights at one end of a long arm to sling heavy boulders high in the air from the other end. Armies used these machines to send showers of rocks and burning straw bales over castle walls until the people inside surrendered.

Jester's Hat Prints

In medieval times, the court of a wealthy knight often had a jester to provide entertainment. It was the job of the court jester to be silly and funny to make everyone laugh. The jester wore a three-pointed hat with bells attached. You can make a jester's hat picture and tell some jokes to make everyone smile.

To make a jester's hat design, you will need

- felt-tip pen
- sheets of craft foam
- scissors
- 2 small boxes
- glue
- brightly colored paint
- disposable food trays
- small pieces of cardstock
- sheet of paper
- pom-poms

1 Using the template on page 31, draw half of a jester's hat on the foam. Cut it out. Use this cutout as a template to draw around and make a second identical shape.

2 Glue the two foam templates on to the sides of the boxes to make the hat shape (as shown here).

3 Squeeze a blob of paint on to the tray.

4 Spread the blob of paint into a thin layer with a piece of cardstock.

5 Dab one half of the jester's hat in the paint.

6 Stamp on to the paper several times. Allow it to dry.

7 Repeat step 4 with another color paint and the second half of the hat. Do not worry about joining the halves up too neatly.

8 Glue the pom-poms to the ends of the points on the hat.

If you were a court jester what funny joke would you tell?

What do you call a knight who is afraid to fight?

Sir Render

Roary the Dragon

According to legend, part of a knight's job was to kill fierce dragons if they attacked people. But this cute sock dragon is far too friendly to attack anyone! You could hang him up in your bedroom to breathe fire on any bad dreams.

To make this cute dragon, you will need

- long sock
- cushion stuffing or clean tights cut into pieces
- felt of different colors
- scissors
- fabric glue
- pins
- 2 polystyrene balls
- blue felt-tip pen
- sheet of craft foam
- needle and thread

1 Fill the sock with the stuffing or shredded tights. You will need to put enough in so that the sock holds its shape.

2 Tie a knot in the open end of the sock.

3 Cut out flame shapes from red, orange, and yellow felt. Glue them together. Glue the flames to the toe of the sock, pushing them in a little way to form a mouth.

4 Cut out two pieces of black felt for nostrils. Glue them on either side of the sock above the mouth.

5 Copy the shape on page 30 to cut out two ears from orange felt. Put a blob of glue in the middle of the straight edge of the shape and pinch it together.

6 With a blob of glue, attach the ears to each side of the heel of the sock. Pin in place until the glue has dried. Remove the pins.

7 Using the blue felt-tip pen, color a blue spot on each of the polystyrene balls.

8 Cut two eyelash shapes from the felt. Glue the eyelashes to the sock on either side of the head, just in front of the ears. Glue a polystyrene ball under each of the lashes.

9 Cut out a pair of foam wings. Glue them to the dragon's back.

10 Ask an adult to push a threaded needle through the dragon near the wings. Knot the end under the head and use the loose end to hang your dragon up.

Your dragon can now fly around, breathing fire as he goes.

George and the Dragon

According to legend, Saint George saved a town—and a beautiful princess—from being terrorized by a fierce dragon. George killed the dragon and rescued the princess. Saint George is the Patron Saint of England.

Jousting

Jousting was a sport for knights. It was a test of nerve and skill between two knights on horseback. Both knights carried long poles, called lances, and charged at each other. The winner was the knight who knocked his opponent off his horse. The knights and their horses wore armor for protection. They also wore colorful tunics made from cloth.

To make a jousting picture, you will need

- tracing paper
- soft pencil
- sheet of paper
- tape
- ballpoint pen
- crayons or paints
- glitter glue

1 Trace the shapes on pages 30–31 on to the tracing paper.

2 Turn the tracing paper over. Using the soft pencil, scribble over the lines, covering them completely.

24

3 Place the tracing paper on the sheet of paper scribble side down. When the picture is in the right place, tape the tracing paper down with a small piece of tape.

4 Draw over all the lines again, this time with the ballpoint pen.

5 Carefully peel off the tape. The outline of the picture will be on the paper.

6 Have fun painting or coloring your picture. Use glitter glue to make it sparkle.

Drawstring Purses

Medieval knights and their ladies kept coins in drawstring purses made of leather or velvet. They often tied these purses to their belts for safe keeping. These snazzy drawstring purses are decorated with colored tassels.

To make a drawstring purse, you will need

- plate 10 in. (25 cm) across the widest part
- fleece or T-shirt fabric (ask permission before you cut up an old T-shirt)
- felt-tip pen
- scissors
- hole punch
- thin ribbon or cord
- glitter glue, scraps of felt or fabric

To make a tassel, you will need

- thin yarn or embroidery thread
- piece of stiff cardboard the length you want the tassel to be
- scissors

Drawstring Purse

1 Place the plate on top of your fabric and draw around it. Cut the circle out.

2 Use the hole punch to make holes around the edge of the fabric, evenly spaced about ¾ in. (2 cm) apart.

3 Thread the ribbon or cord into one hole and out of the next all the way around the circle. Pull the ribbon or cord to gather up the top of the bag.

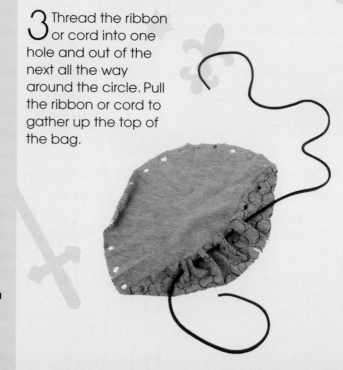

Tassel

1 Wrap the yarn or thread around the cardboard 30 times. Cut the yarn.

2 Cut a piece of yarn about 6 in. (15 cm) long. Slide it under the yarn at the top of the cardboard. Tie it tightly in a knot.

3 Cut through all the loops at the bottom of the cardbaord.

4 Cut a piece of yarn 8 in. (20 cm) long. Wrap it tightly around the yarn just below the knot and tie it. Trim the ends. Trim the bottom of the tassel to even up the ends. Tie the tassel on to the bag through one of the holes.

You could make a lovely present by filling one of these pouches with candy.

To make a striped tassel, wrap three different colors of embroidery thread around the cardboard.

This bag is printed to look like chainmail—see page 14 to find out how to do this. You will need to stamp the fabric before making the bag. The cord is a leather shoelace. The chainmail bag would make a great addition to the knight's outfit on page 14.

Castle Picture

In some old churches or castles you might find engraved brass portraits of medieval knights. In recent times, it became a popular hobby to make copies of these pictures by laying sheets of paper on top and gently rubbing across the paper with pencil or wax. You can make your own rubbing pictures using everyday objects from around the house.

For this rubbing picture, you will need

- materials with different textures such as string, coins, leaves, stickers, safety pins, paperclips, lentils, spaghetti
- scraps of paper
- wax crayons
- cardboard
- glue
- sheet of thin paper

1 To make a rubbing, place a sheet of paper on top of your chosen object and gently rub the wax crayon across the paper. Try a few rubbings on scraps of paper to see which objects work best.

2 Corrugated cardboard has a stripy texture.

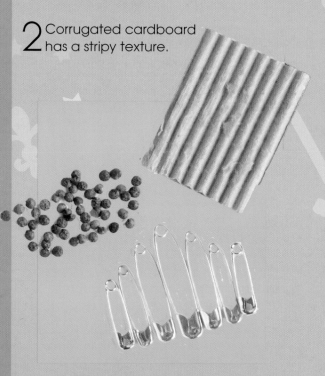

3 Paperclips and safety pins make interesting shapes and patterns. You can create great textures with lentil or rice rubbings.

4 Pieces of spaghetti are good for making straight outlines.

5 Leaf rubbings make great pictures. In a scene, they look like miniature trees.

6 String can be used to make curved outlines and curly shapes like this sun. The texture in the center is made by rubbing over a small coin.

7 A rubbing made from overlapping stickers looks like bricks or stones.

8 When you have collected all the elements you need for your picture, stick them on to a piece of cardboard. Place a sheet of paper on top and gently rub different colored wax crayons over the objects to reveal your magic picture.

Templates

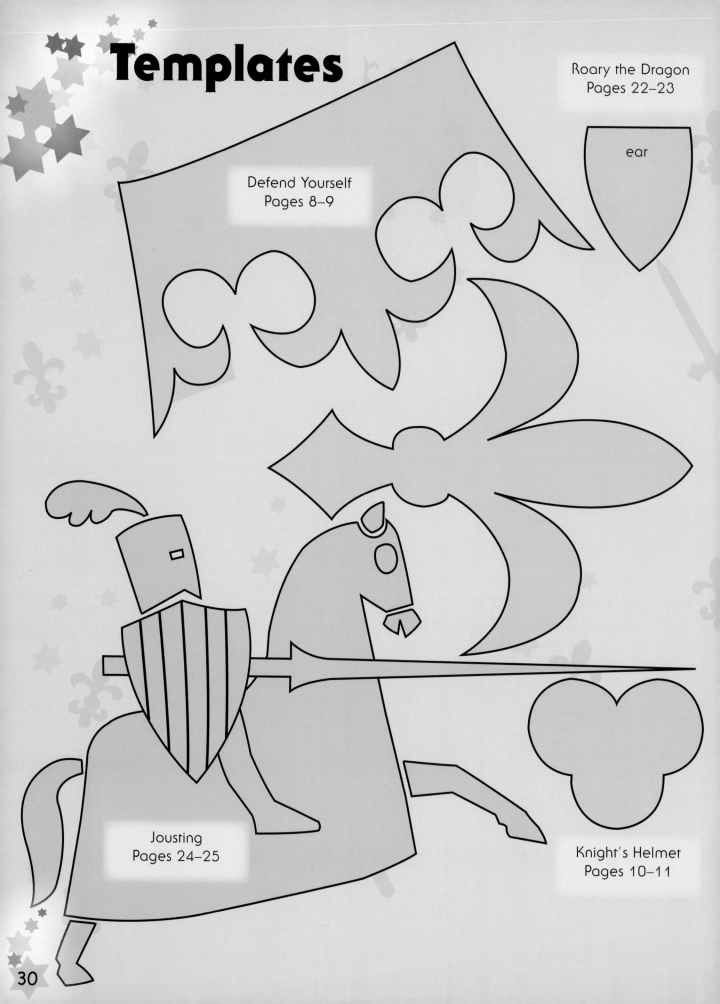

Roary the Dragon
Pages 22–23

ear

Defend Yourself
Pages 8–9

Jousting
Pages 24–25

Knight's Helmet
Pages 10–11

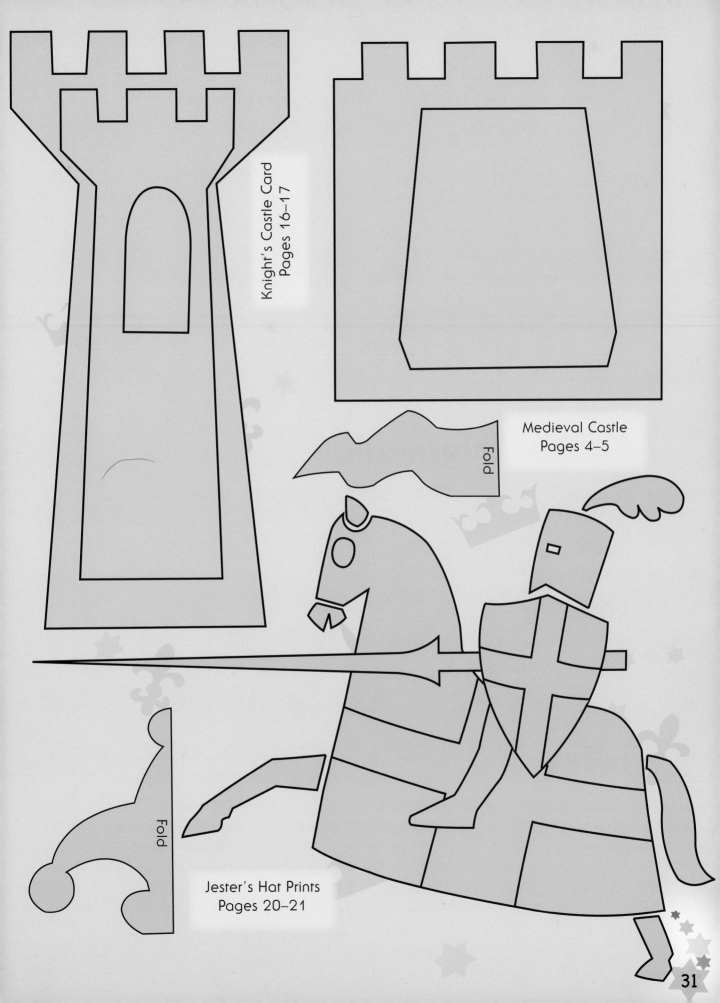

Knight's Castle Card
Pages 16–17

Medieval Castle
Pages 4–5

Fold

Fold

Jester's Hat Prints
Pages 20–21

31

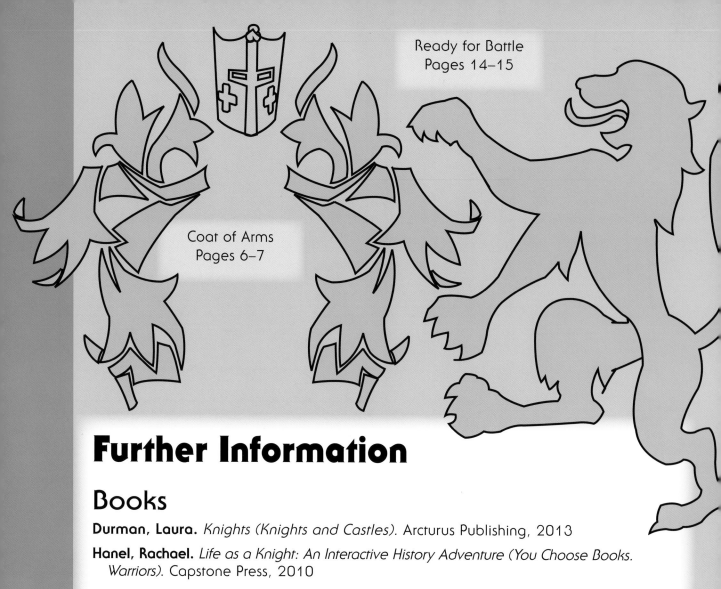

Coat of Arms
Pages 6–7

Ready for Battle
Pages 14–15

Further Information

Books

Durman, Laura. *Knights (Knights and Castles).* Arcturus Publishing, 2013

Hanel, Rachael. *Life as a Knight: An Interactive History Adventure (You Choose Books. Warriors).* Capstone Press, 2010

Websites

http://www.kathimitchell.com/middleages.htm

http://medievaleurope.mrdonn.org/heraldry.html

Index